MEXICO
Leading the Southern Hemisphere

ZESTY AND COLORFUL CUISINE
THE FOOD OF MEXICO

A Mexican woman buys tortillas from a vendor in Mexico City. Mexicans consume an estimated 30,000 tons of tortillas a day, 65 percent of which are hand made using traditional methods.

MEXICO
Leading the Southern Hemisphere

ZESTY AND COLORFUL CUISINE
THE FOOD OF MEXICO

MASON CREST
PHILADELPHIA

Mason Crest
450 Parkway Drive, Suite D
Broomall, PA 19008
www.masoncrest.com

Printed and bound in the United States of America.

CPSIA Compliance Information: Batch #M2014.
For further information, contact Mason Crest at 1-866-MCP-Book.

First printing

1 3 5 7 9 8 6 4 2

Library of Congress Cataloging-in-Publication Data
      on file at the Library of Congress

        ISBN: 978-1-4222-3222-4 (hc)
        ISBN: 978-1-4222-8687-6 (ebook)

Mexico: Leading the Southern Hemisphere series ISBN: 978-1-4222-3213-2

TABLE OF CONTENTS

	Timeline	8
1.	Aztec Treasures	11
2.	The Incredible Tortilla	23
3.	Spanish Influences	31
4.	Feasts and Fiestas	41
5.	Five Meals a Day—and Between-Meal Whims	51
	Series Glossary	58
	Further Reading	59
	Internet Resources	60
	Index	62
	About the Author	64

MEXICO

Leading the Southern Hemisphere

BEAUTIFUL DIVERSITY: THE GEOGRAPHY OF MEXICO

FAMOUS PEOPLE OF MEXICAN HISTORY

SPIRIT OF A NATION: THE PEOPLE OF MEXICO

FIESTA! THE FESTIVALS OF MEXICO

**ANCIENT LAND WITH A FASCINATING PAST:
THE HISTORY OF MEXICO**

**VITAL AND CREATIVE:
THE ART AND ARCHITECTURE OF MEXICO**

VICTORIA! THE SPORTS OF MEXICO

FINDING A FINANCIAL BALANCE: THE ECONOMY OF MEXICO

ZESTY AND COLORFUL CUISINE: THE FOOD OF MEXICO

**MEETING FUTURE CHALLENGES:
THE GOVERNMENT OF MEXICO**

MEXICO'S GULF STATES

MEXICO'S PACIFIC NORTH STATES

MEXICO'S PACIFIC SOUTH STATES

MEXICO'S NORTHERN STATES

MEXICO'S CENTRAL STATES

MEXICAN FACTS AND FIGURES

KEY ICONS TO LOOK FOR:

 Text-dependent questions: These questions send the reader back to the text for more careful attention to the evidence presented there.

 Words to understand: These words with their easy-to-understand definitions will increase the reader's understanding of the text, while building vocabulary skills.

 Series glossary of key terms: This back-of-the book glossary contains terminology used throughout this series. Words found here increase the reader's ability to read and comprehend higher-level books and articles in this field.

 Research projects: Readers are pointed toward areas of further inquiry connected to each chapter. Suggestions are provided for projects that encourage deeper research and analysis.

 Sidebars: This boxed material within the main text allows readers to build knowledge, gain insights, explore possibilities, and broaden their perspectives by weaving together additional information to provide realistic and holistic perspectives.

TIMELINE

250 B.C–A.D 750	Tamales are invented.
1325	Tenochtitlán is built.
1519	Aztecs honor Spanish conquistadors with a banquet.
1521	Spanish conquer Mexico. Roman Catholic missionaries bring new ingredients, recipes, and cooking methods.
1530	Spanish bring domestic cattle to Mexico and establish ranches.
1680s	Spanish nuns create the Mexican national dish, *molé poblano de guajolote*.
1821	Mexico wins independence.
1863	French occupy Mexico. Breads and pastries become popular.
1867	French leave Mexico.
1859	First corn mill registered.
1890s	Electric corn mills operate.
1899	First tortilla machine patented.
1902	First tortilla factory opens.
1910	Mexican Revolution begins.
1917	Mexican government divides private estates into small farms.
1940s	Traditional dishes regain respectability as Mexican national cuisine.
1966	Frito-Lay begins to make tortilla chips.
1985	First McDonald's opens in Mexico.
1990	Tortillas marketed in United States.

8

1998 Mexican government enriches tortilla flour with vitamins and minerals.

2001 Mexican government requires that tortillas be made from only white corn.

2006 Public health experts express worry about the increasing popularity of imported ramen noodles, which are less nutritious than traditional Mexican meals.

2007 A sudden jump in the cost of corn tortillas leads to nationwide protests.

2008 President Felipe Calderón considers reducing taxes and trade barriers to halt the rising prices of basic food items.

2009 The Mexican government permits some large agribusinesses to plant trial plots of genetically modified corn in Mexico.

2013 The Mexican government bans the planting or selling of genetically modified corn in the country.

2014 A U.N. study finds that Mexico has the highest adult obesity rate in the world, with about one-third of adult Mexicans having a body mass index (BMI) that is above the standards for overweight or obese.

Huevos rancheros is a popular breakfast in Mexico. It consists of fried eggs served on a lightly fried corn tortilla, and accompanied by a tomato-chili sauce.

WORDS TO UNDERSTAND

ambassador—an authorized representative of a country who travels in friendship to another nation.

chafing dish—a container used to keep food warm at the table.

conquistadors—Spanish conquerors of the New World.

cuisine—style of cooking.

enchiladas—tortillas wrapped around seasoned, shredded meat, cheese or beans, then baked or fried and dipped in or topped with spicy sauce.

molé—a thick sauce of ground chilies and seasonings for stewing meat.

quesadillas—tortillas folded over a filling, then grilled.

smallpox—a contagious disease that causes high fevers and pus-filled sores that leave deep scars.

tamale—cornmeal dough stuffed with spicy meat, wrapped in corn husks, and steamed.

tortilla—a round, thin bread made of unleavened cornmeal or wheat flour.

Tacos, such as the ones shown at left, are among Mexico's most recognized dishes.

AZTEC TREASURES

It's been said Mexican cooks can turn the most meager ingredients into pure gold. Mexico boasts one of the oldest forms of original cooking, dating back to the Aztec civilization. Since those ancient times, Mexicans' skill and imagination have transformed simple foods into culinary treasures. Through hard work and precision, corn becomes **tortillas** and **tamales**. Beans simmer into hardy stews. Chilies add unique flavors to rich sauces.

At home and in restaurants, Americans today enjoy meals based on genuine Mexican **cuisine**. But these Americanized versions of Mexican foods resemble the originals only slightly. Restaurant owners who offer food too authentic to satisfy American tastes find staying in business difficult.

As Mexican food manufacturer Francisco "Frank" Morales explains, Americans like Mexican dishes made with ground beef, while true Mexican cooks use center cuts of beef, pork, mutton, goat, chicken, and turkey. Also,

EASY GUACAMOLE

2 large avocados, peeled and pits removed
2 teaspoons lemon juice
$^1/_3$ cup salsa

1. *In medium bowl, mash avocados with a fork.*
2. *Add lemon juice and salsa; stir until blended.*
3. *Refrigerate until serving. Makes approximately 1$^1/_2$ cups.*

most Americans prefer sweet tomato-based sauces to traditional bitter chili sauces. The menu of a Mexican-style restaurant in the United States might center on tacos, **enchiladas**, and **quesadillas**. In Mexico, these items, known as *antojitos*, are eaten as snacks or appetizers.

The Mexican food we know today is rooted in native food thousands of years ago. Corn (or maize) was domesticated in Mexico around 9,000 years ago in the region of modern Guerrero and in the Balsas River valley. Eventually, maize was planted by people throughout Mexico and the American southwest. Some 4,000 years ago the Olmec and Maya civilizations domesticated beans, and chili peppers and developed the flatbread cakes known as tortillas. After conquering most of central Mexico around the year 1,400 C.E., the Aztecs expanded the Mexican diet by introducing other meats, fruits, and vegetables. After 1519, as the Spanish conquered and colonized Mexico, European cooks brought new ingredients, recipes, and food preparation methods. Traditional Amerindian foods took new twists.

The tortilla is an excellent example of these changes. The native Amerindians ate these flat cakes made from corn dough alone or used them as the basis for more complex dishes. After the Spanish imported wheat, tortillas made with flour instead of ground corn became one of the first innovations. Flour tortillas remain popular throughout modern Mexico, especially in the north.

Throughout Mexico's 300 years as a Spanish colony, Europeans, Americans, Asians, and other ethnic groups influenced the native Mexican cuisine. This gradual blending of heritages is known as *mestizaje*. Most native people enjoyed the same foods their ancestors had eaten, but European cooking reigned as the preference of the upper classes. Not until the 1940s, well after winning independence, did Mexicans begin reviving old recipes and claiming their own national cuisine.

A Mexican woman cooks tortillas in her home. The corn tortillas bake on a sheet over an open flame, while a pot of seasoned rice or meat is prepared as a filling.

The writings of Spanish explorer Hernán Cortés and the men who traveled with him reveal much about how the Aztecs lived. Tales of Aztec wealth first drew Cortés to Tenochtitlán, the Aztecs' capital city. Cortés landed along Mexico's Yucatán coast in March 1519 and conquered the town of Tabasco. Natives there described the riches of the Aztec empire. Excited by their stories, Cortés continued his quest.

The Aztec empire was highly advanced in many ways. The Aztecs had built on knowledge from earlier native cultures to become skilled in art, astronomy, mathematics, writing, calendars, music, sculpture, metalwork, textiles and weaving, architecture, and farming. Aztec farmers irrigated their fields with canal systems. In orchards they grew avocados, coconuts, papayas, and pineapples. They raised green tomatoes, chilies, sweet potatoes, squash, peanuts, beans, and herbs, but kept few domestic animals.

 The peanut was known to the Aztecs as *tlalcachuatl*, "earth peanut." Today's Spanish word for peanut—*cacahuate*—comes from this ancient Aztec word.

While the nobles enjoyed a lavish lifestyle, most natives lived simply. They wore cotton clothing and built wood or stone houses. Unlike the rulers who ate meat or fish, common people survived on a vegetarian diet, mainly corn. They ate corn tortillas and flavored cornmeal porridge called *atole*; beans seasoned with chilies, bananas, and wild papaya; and guacamole made from avocados. They drank *pulque*, an alcoholic beverage made from the partially fermented sap of the maguey cactus plant.

The ancient Mexicans offered sacrifices to certain gods to ensure a bountiful harvest. This statue is a representation of Xilonen, a seasonal goddess.

16

Meanwhile, Aztec rulers feasted on elaborate banquets including stewed meats in chili sauce or *molé*, fried bananas, boiled nopal cactus, and tamales. Nobles achieved fame and status by serving tortillas, stew, and hot or cold chocolate drinks to their guests. Their cooks shaped tortillas like butterflies or leaves. Food for feasts stayed warm in *chafing dishes*. The Aztecs observed certain table manners, holding tortillas properly, using cotton napkins, and not stuffing their mouths or slurping. Music and dancing frequently ended a banquet. Occasionally, royal feasts served as charity to feed the poor.

Because the Aztecs depended on nature for survival, it is not surprising they worshiped the sun. Food, especially corn, which originated in Mexico, was considered a gift from the gods. According to Mayan and Aztec myths, the gods had molded humans from corn dough. To ensure a good harvest, ancient people did whatever they believed necessary to keep their gods happy, strong, and generous so their crops would grow.

At a festival held during the dry season, the Aztecs asked Chicomecóatl (also called Xilonen), the goddess of sustenance, to bless seed corn. Depicted as a young woman in red wearing a tiara, corn necklace, and holding ears of corn, she was associated with abundance and fertility. To honor the goddess, maidens danced on flower petals in the fields. The god Centéotl reigned over the harvest.

Some Aztec religious offerings involved human sacrifices. Sometimes they killed prisoners of war or slaves as sacrifices, and for such cruelty other tribes feared and hated them.

Founded in 1325, the Aztec capital, Tenochtitlán, occupied an island in Lake Texcoco. Linked to the mainland by causeways and

From the maguey cactus, also called Mexican aloe, Aztecs made beverages, sweeteners, fabric, paper, needles and pins, and shingles for their houses.

Tamales are a popular food for meals and snacks in Mexico. They consist of cornhusks filled with cornmeal dough and a mixture of fried meat and peppers.

18

Snake head carvings decorate the temple of Quetzalcoatl in the citadel of Teotihuacan. A major creator god of the Aztecs and Toltecs, Quetzalcoatl is said to have introduced agriculture to Mexico.

protected by dams, Tenochtitlán was a city of large houses, palaces, and pyramids. Every day, the market brought in some 60,000 vendors and shoppers. They bartered for pottery, fabrics, arrows, tools, and food in exchange for gold, stamped tin, or cocoa beans.

Aztec Emperor Montezuma II, the ninth Aztec king, ruled from 1502 to 1520. Known as a harsh tyrant, when he learned of the Spaniards' landing, he contemplated how to act toward them. Montezuma believed Cortés was connected to Quetzalcoatl, a light-skinned, bearded Aztec god predicted to return in the year of the Spaniards' arrival. Dressed in jewels, feathers, and gold, Montezuma and about 200 nobles marching in two columns met Cortés and his men as they reached the city's entrance. The blending of Amerindian and European heritage began here, as two cultures with contrasting customs, religion, and beliefs came together for the first time. A Spanish-speaking native woman named La Malinche—called Doña Marina by the Spaniards—acted as interpreter.

In a peaceful gesture, the two leaders exchanged necklaces. Cortés assured Montezuma he came as an **ambassador**. The emperor promised Cortés anything he asked. Montezuma welcomed the Spanish as honored guests. They shared a lavish banquet of turkey stew and white tortillas, and Montezuma invited Cortés to stay in the palace. In return, Cortés took Montezuma hostage.

The Aztecs drove the Spanish from Tenochititlán in a battle known as *la noche triste*, the sorrowful night. But the Spanish possessed better weapons and battle strategy. Montezuma's savagery toward conquered tribes prompted other Amerindians, especially the Tlascalans, to fight with the Spanish. The **conquistadors** also brought **smallpox**, and many Aztecs died from the previously unknown disease. By 1521, the Spanish had defeated the Aztecs. Cortés occupied and destroyed Tenochititlán. He later founded Mexico City on the site.

Mexico remained a Spanish colony until 1821. The Spanish had come to Mexico not only for wealth, but to spread the Roman Catholic religion. As friars, monks, priests, and nuns brought Christianity, European customs and cookery accompanied them. But Mexico's original native cuisine formed the foundation for all later Mexican cooking. Names of many modern Mexican dishes stem from words in the Aztec language, Nahuatl.

Montezuma enjoyed frozen confections flavored with fruit or chocolate. He was said to have sent runners up a mountain to bring ice for his treats.

Because life in ancient Mexico depended on preparing food in addition to growing it, the native Mexicans had developed clever ways to process food. They invented equipment for mashing and grilling and found ways to season food and make it taste better. Without the convenience of electric appliances, cooking was very hard work.

Using the *metate*, a flat, slanted grinding stone, they ground chilies, tomatoes, cornmeal, or pumpkinseeds into thick sauces they called *molli*. Seasoned beans simmered slowly in clay pots, *cazuelas*, set over hot coals. Mashing chilies and tart fruits called *tomatillos* with avocado flavored their guacamole. Wrapping food in leaves gave it a special flavor while roasting. Tamales were steamed in cornhusks. Other foods were roasted in banana leaves or maguey leaves.

The history of Mexican food comes to us in many ways. We know what the Aztecs ate from descriptions written by Cortés and his companions, who were astonished by all they saw. We also know about the Aztecs' cuisine because it is still practiced. Through the centuries, residents of small villages have continued making tortillas and tamales in the old way. Chefs and cookbook authors have visited Mexican communities to research recipes passed down through generations. In addition, modern researchers can identify ingredients used in ancient foods by studying residue on pottery fragments.

 Before humans learned to cultivate crops, they survived by hunting and gathering wild plants. Ancient Mexicans began farming at least 8,000 years ago. After analyzing seeds discovered in a Mexican cave, scientists determined early varieties of pumpkins and summer squash were grown as crops.

Before his captivity, Montezuma's diet reflected his power and prestige as emperor. He feasted daily on hundreds of dishes prepared by his servants. In his banquet hall, the Spanish sampled foods made from ingredients they had never tasted before. Here and in the market, the newcomers saw tortillas, tamales, wild turkey, quail, duck, frogs, newts, lobsters, corn, squash, beans, avocado, tomatoes, squash, cactus, shrimp, herring, partridge, and other Aztec delights.

Drinking chocolate, one of Montezuma's favorite treats, represented the ultimate indulgence, reserved only for nobles. The Aztecs prized cacao beans so much they used them as money. To make a hot or cold beverage, they ground the beans, known to them as *xoxoc-atl*, into powder. They added water, honey, and flavorings such as vanilla or pepper. Unlike the hot chocolate we enjoy on a wintry day, this drink contained no sugar and no milk. The Spanish quickly grew fond of chocolate, but after it was imported to Europe, a controversy arose over whether it was too decadent and might corrupt those who drank it. Hundreds of years later, the English began preparing cocoa with milk.

TEXT-DEPENDENT QUESTIONS

When and where was maize (corn) domesticated in Mexico?

How do present-day people know what Aztecs ate 500 years ago?

RESEARCH PROJECT

In some parts of Mexico, to ensure fertility and good rainfall, a ceremony called the Dance of the Voladores is done during the summertime. (You can search for and view videos of the Voladores on YouTube.) Do some research into this ceremony, and find out more about what the Voladores do, and why. Present your findings to the class.

 WORDS TO UNDERSTAND

frontier—the unsettled region at the edge of a civilization.

lime—a caustic, white powder made of calcium hydroxide.

staple—the chief commodity or food of a particular people or region.

Tortillas are an important part of the Mexican diet, and there is a movement to make them more nutritious. Corn flour used to make the tortillas is now enriched with soy, vitamins, and minerals in an effort to improve the health of impoverished children.

THE INCREDIBLE TORTILLA

The invention of the tortilla constitutes one of the ancient world's most amazing cooking feats. From plain corn, the Aztecs created a versatile flat bread with lasting appeal. The Spanish called these *tortillas*, which means "small cake." Tortillas packed easily for a journey or festival. Folded, they wrapped other foods or made an edible scoop for stew or beans. Flat, they formed a makeshift platter. Cooked into a crisp tostada, they stayed fresh for a long time. Centuries later, on America's western *frontier*, tortillas became favored camp chow after Mexican vaqueros introduced them to the other cowboys.

Although tortillas were introduced to supermarkets throughout the United States only within the past 60 years, today they enjoy global popularity. Frito-Lay first marketed tortilla chips in 1966. Ready-made tortillas for home cooking didn't become generally available in American stores until 1990. They caught on so fast that by 1996 Americans were eating more than 64 billion a year. That figure has only grown since then. By 2014, the sale of tortillas and related products, such as tortilla chips, taco shells, and tostada shells, exceeded $6 billion a year.

According to legend, a Mayan peasant invented the tortilla for his king.

Today, American shoppers buy more tortillas than any other ethnic and specialty breads, including muffins, bagels, croissants, and hot dog or hamburger rolls. Varieties flavored with spinach, tomato, or garlic are gaining popularity. Tortillas have even traveled to outer space, feeding NASA astronauts.

Making corn tortillas is no simple task. The process requires time, patience, physical strength, and skill. First, the corn must soak overnight in water containing **lime**. This process, called *nixtamalización*, softens the corn kernels so the outer shells can be removed. It also slightly changes the corn's flavor. The Aztecs used lime from oyster shells and other seashells and from limestone. What they didn't know was that soaking the corn in lime also released amino acids and made the corn more nutritious. Once softened, the corn is ground into dough called *masa*, which can then be rolled and shaped to make tortillas, tamales, and other foods.

TORTILLAS DE HARINA (FLOUR TORTILLAS)

2 cups flour
1 teaspoon salt
$^1/_3$ cup vegetable shortening
$^1/_2$ cup warm water

1. *Mix together flour and salt in a bowl.*
2. *Cut in the shortening, then add water to make a stiff dough.*
3. *Knead on a lightly floured board.*
4. *Form dough into 8 small balls.*
5. *Let dough stand 15 minutes.*
6. *With a heavy wooden rolling pin, roll balls to paper-thin thickness and brown in a lightly greased skillet. Turn with spatula.*
7. *Eat or cool, then store in a sealed plastic bag.*

Rolling out tortillas is a delicate process that requires a great deal of practice and skill. It is important that the tortillas be neither too thick nor too thin, or they will not cook as well.

24

A man buys tortillas from a vendor in Mexico City. Since 2007, the Mexican government has attempted to set the market price for tortillas, as a way to ensure that poor families will be able to afford this staple of the Mexican diet.

26

Until the advent of corn mills and the widespread implementation of mass production techniques in the 1950s, tortillas continued to be made by hand as in ancient times. Women took charge of making fresh tortillas to feed their families. Each morning, they knelt at metates, grinding corn into dough. If the paste turned out too thick or thin, it might fold or tear as it was patted, clapped, and turned into the proper shape and thickness. Once formed, the flat pancakes were cooked on a hot *comal*, a flat charcoal griddle with a curved edge. After the tortilla cooked on one side, it was turned with a flick of the fingers. Tortillas constitute such an important part of the Mexican diet that, according to superstition, burning a tortilla means bad luck.

At one time, medicinal herbs were added to tortilla dough in hopes of making it more wholesome. Because tortillas remain a **staple** for many Mexicans, in September 1998, the government instituted a program to increase their nutritional value. President Ernesto Zedillo announced a plan requiring the addition of iron, zinc, and vitamins to corn and wheat flour.

Attempts to invent a mechanical corn mill that would eliminate grinding corn by hand began in the middle 1800s. By the 1890s, electric corn mills operated throughout Mexico. During this era, several inventors attempted to design a tortilla press. The first tortilla machine was patented in 1899, and Mexico's first tortilla factory opened in 1902. Even *tortillerías*, Mexican stores specializing in tortillas, ultimately switched from selling handmade tortillas to mass-produced ones.

Tortillas are manufactured through a process beginning with ground masa poured into a bin, then mixed into dough. Stamped tortillas pop out through a press at the bottom.

A Mexican woman uses a hinged board to press corn dough into a tortilla, circa 1940. Even today, many people use traditional methods to make tortillas.

28

Tortillas can be baked or fried until crispy chips and served with salsa, a snack that Americans have adopted from Mexico.

They travel along a conveyor belt over a hot flame in an oven, flip over to cook on the other side, then fall into a basket.

In Mexico, more people are now buying manufactured tortillas in supermarkets. Ready-made tortillas provide convenience, but they may not taste as good as the homemade ones do. In most parts of Mexico, shoppers who prefer the taste of fresh handmade tortillas, but don't have time to make them, can purchase them in markets or from vendors.

Although corn tortillas remain the most popular, tortillas made from wheat flour are becoming more common, especially in northern Mexico. Flour tortillas are somewhat easier to make than corn tortillas, because the dough can be rolled into disks instead of patted by hand. Keeping them small makes the dough easier to handle. Perfect tortillas require practice. Developing the knack takes a few tries.

In recent years, the Mexican government has wrestled with the issue of genetically modified (GMO) corn. In 2001, the government ruled that GMO corn could not be used in food sold in Mexico. However, in 2009 the government permitted several large agribusinesses to plant small amounts of GMO corn. In 2013, the government reversed this decision, ruling that GMO corn could not be planted in the country, and that tortillas sold commercially in Mexico had to be made from non-GMO corn. However, many people believe that the government will eventually reverse this stance due to high demand for corn.

Inventor Luis Romero Soto was born in San Juan del Río in 1876. As a boy, he fashioned an alarm clock from a string, candle, and kitchen utensils to wake himself up for school. As a teenager, he invented an automatic postage machine. Although he made his living designing ironwork for mansions, he invented and patented a tortilla machine. Afterward, he opened the first tortilla factory and began mass marketing manufactured tortillas.

29

TEXT-DEPENDENT QUESTIONS

What type of grain were tortillas originally made from?

In what decade of the 20th century did mass-production of tortillas become widespread?

RESEARCH PROJECT

In recent decades scientists have attempted to develop new strains of food, including corn, that are resistant to drought and disease, or that produce higher yields when harvested. In some cases, specific genes from one type of plant are inserted into another plant to produce the desired trait. However, some people are concerned that genetically altered food may not be safe for human consumption. Using the Internet, do some research on the pros and cons of GMO food. Write a report making the case for or against consumption of GMO food by humans. Use scientific studies and other research to support your conclusions.

Marzipan is a confection made from crushed almonds or almond paste, sugar, and egg whites, then formed into decorative, and often colorful, shapes. Marzipan cookies are particularly popular at Christmastime.

SPANISH INFLUENCES

Monks and nuns arriving in New Spain to spread Christianity brought with them European cooking techniques. The nuns were smart, resourceful, and educated in domestic skills—like embroidery, needlepoint, and cooking. Their convent kitchen innovations mixed Spanish and Amerindian cuisine to create new fare.

Back in early colonial days, religious orders made the first impact on native cookery, although their real mission was to convert natives. By the end of Spanish rule, millions of natives had accepted the Catholic religion.

In addition to their religious duties, nuns prepared confections to earn income for their orders or as gifts for influential officials. They did this so expertly, many convents became well known for their candies, custards, puddings, and other sweets. The Santa Rosa Convent in Puebla grew famous for *camotes*, long strips of candied sweet potatoes. In Mexico City, the Convent of San Francisco specialized in *aleluyas*, almond and cinnamon candies given as Easter presents. Other convents earned reputations for chocolates, **marzipan**, or jam-filled crescents called *fruta de horno*. Nuns mixed Old World and New World ingredients and skills to create these goodies.

Frequently in Mexico today, candy is served as dessert, but the custom of

32

eating dessert after a meal comes from Europe. When the sisters lacked ingredients for a favorite recipe they brought with them, they substituted native foods. The Spanish brought milk, eggs, sugar, and almonds, and they made use of Mexican chocolate, coconut, and other fruits and nuts. The Aztecs sweetened dishes with honey or cactus juice. The Spanish brought and planted sugar, which thrived in the tropical regions.

In their gardens, the sisters planted seeds and cuttings of Old World plants, carrots, onions, peas, cabbage, to see what would grow in the Mexican climate. Not all plants could survive. They found concocting a heavy paste or jam known as *ate* preserved fruit in the tropical climate. Sometimes, the nuns requested help from native women familiar with the local foods.

The most famous legend in all Mexican cooking history centers on an original stew created by a Spanish nun. Her *molé poblano de guajolote*, or turkey in molé sauce, became

MOLLETES DE CALABAZA (PUMPKIN MUFFINS)

1 cup canned pumpkin
$1/2$ cup milk
1 egg, well-beaten
$1/2$ cup sugar
2 tablespoons melted margarine
1 teaspoon nutmeg
1 teaspoon cinnamon
$1^1/2$ cups flour
1 teaspoon salt
3 teaspoons baking powder

1. *Preheat the oven to 400°F (204°C)*
2. *Mix the pumpkin and milk, then add the egg, sugar, melted margarine, and spices.*
3. *In a separate mixing bowl, stir the flour, salt, and baking powder together.*
4. *Stir the dry ingredients into the pumpkin mixture.*
5. *Pour into greased muffin tins, filling them about half full, and bake 25 minutes.*

Makes about 12 muffins.

Many Mexicans buy their food from street vendors rather than from grocery stores. The food available in the street markets, such as these blackberries and chilies, are fresher and less expensive than prepackaged food.

34

A woman grills fresh corn on the cob at a market stall in Mexico. Corn is probably the most important crop in the traditional Mexican diet, as it can be used in almost any dish. Scientists believe corn evolved from wild grains that cross-pollinated by chance some 10,000 years ago, and was eventually domesticated by ancient Amerindian residents of Mexico.

Mexico's national dish. Festive fare, *molé poblano* comes in many variations and is served at all celebrations.

As the story goes, one day in the 1680s, Sor Andrea de la Asunción of the Santa Rosa convent in Puebla de los Angeles hoped to prepare an unforgettable meal to impress a visiting dignitary, either an archbishop or a viceroy. As she began cooking, she cut up and boiled a turkey with tomatoes. Employing native methods, she toasted red and black chilies, then ground them into paste on a *metate*. As the mixture simmered, she added cloves, cinnamon, peppercorns, coriander, sesame seeds, other seasonings, and ground tortillas. As a final inspiration, she added chocolate. She may have hoped the chocolate would tone down the spiciness or maybe she simply wanted to make her creation unique. One variation of the legend says that Sor Andrea accidentally spilled an entire tray of spices into the pot where the *molé* was cooking, creating the unique blend of flavors.

Accident or not, the important visitor approved. Spanish missionaries

MEXICAN WEDDING CAKES

$1/2$ **pound butter**
$1/2$ **cup sugar**
1 teaspoon vanilla
green food coloring
2 cups sifted all-purpose flour
1 cup pecans, finely chopped
confectioners' sugar

1. *Cream the butter. Add the sugar and vanilla; cream until light and fluffy.*
2. *Add a few drops of food coloring to tint a light green.*
3. *Add the flour and pecans; mix well.*
4. *Roll into one-inch balls and place an inch apart on an ungreased cookie sheet.*
5. *Bake in an oven heated to 325°F (163°C) for 18 to 20 minutes, or until lightly browned.*
6. *Remove from the cookie sheet and roll in confectioners' sugar while warm. Makes about $4^1/2$ dozen balls.*

36

A plate of molé poblano sauce over a turkey leg, which has been called Mexico's "national dish." It is also commonly eaten in the state of Puebla during the annual Cinco de Mayo celebration.

began serving *molé poblano* at religious celebrations, and the dish became a favorite throughout Mexico. The idea of chocolate chili sauce on turkey may sound unappetizing if you imagine a candy bar melted in stew. But what is actually used is a tiny piece of unsweetened Mexican chocolate.

Despite *molé poblano's* popularity, recipes for it weren't printed until the middle 1800s. Preparing *molé poblano* presents a major task. It requires at least eight hours, usually over several days, and from 20 to 30 ingredients, depending on the recipe. Chilies must be roasted, spices ground. At **fiesta** time, residents of some towns used to set up an assembly line to make molé. Today, commercially made molés have become

Wild turkey got its name from 16th-century Europeans, who mistakenly believed the imported birds had come from Turkey rather than Mexico.

A vendor sells fresh bread in a market in Monterrey.

more popular in Mexico, because most people are too busy to make it the traditional way.

The Spanish also changed the way native Mexicans ate by importing the first domestic animals to Mexico. The Spaniards brought cattle, pigs, chickens, sheep, goats, horses, donkeys, and mules. Conquistadors obtained land grants to create ranches where they raised their cattle. Eventually, the natives acquired a taste for beef, pork, and chicken, and worked them into their own traditional recipes. For example, they began making tamales with pork fat.

The Spanish liked breads baked with wheat flour, the kind they had eaten at home. Because the Catholic Church considered wheat the only acceptable grain for Communion wafers, efforts to replace native grains with wheat flour became a religious matter. The Europeans also believed wheat provided more nutrition than corn. The natives loved corn, however, and at first the Spanish couldn't even give wheat bread away to beggars. Colonists planted

White pozole (pozole blanco) is a Mexican soup that is popular in many states, particularly Sinaloa, Michoacán, Guerrero, Jalisco, and Morelos.

wheat fields, though, and eventually, the Amerindians who tended them ate the bread they received as wages.

Early in Mexico's history, bakeries were held in low regard. Criminals were forced to work there as punishment. As a result of French influences after the Spanish occupation ended, however, wonderful bakeries flourish throughout Mexico today. Shoppers choose from an assortment of rolls, *crêpes*, pastries, breads, and sweet breads. Traditional wheat bread is baked in a brick oven with a wood fire and contains no preservatives.

The Spanish also brought to Mexico the process of sautéing or frying foods in fats. They exported native Mexican foods—pineapple, wild turkey, cocoa, sweet potatoes, squash, pumpkins and peanuts—to Europe.

 The native Mexicans categorized hot peppers as ají and sweet peppers as chilies.

Many convents shut down in the 19th and 20th centuries as the church lost its influence in Mexico.

The church's increasing wealth and power had triggered reforms against church control, and the government implemented restrictions against the church. Under Mexico's 1857 constitution the church could no longer own property, and the convent in

 The Spanish brought and cultivated the radish during the colonial days. Today, radishes are often carved into roses to garnish Mexican dishes. In Oaxaca, an annual Christmas celebration, Night of the Radishes, features sculptures shaped from long red radishes, flowers, and dried cornhusks.

Puebla closed. Today, it is a national monument. Puebla remains Mexico's candy capital, famed for sweet shops offering marzipan molded into various shapes, candied figs, guava paste, and of course *camotes*.

 ## TEXT-DEPENDENT QUESTIONS

Who is credited with creating molé poblano?

What are some of the domestic animals brought to Mexico by the Spanish?

 ## RESEARCH PROJECT

As conquistadores added new lands in North America to the Spanish empire during the 15th, 16th, and 17th centuries, the Spaniards attempted to colonize and control the population by converting them to the Roman Catholic religion. To do this, they established religious centers known as missions, especially in rural or frontier areas. The missions were staffed by religious leaders, such as priests and nuns, as well as soldiers to protect them. Read more about the Spanish missions, and write a report explaining the important role they played in spreading Spanish culture and cuisine throughout Mexico, as well as in introducing Mexican food to Europeans.

WORDS TO UNDERSTAND

buñuelos—thin, sugar-coated pancakes or fritters popular at Christmas.

jícama—an edible, starchy root.

4

The Day of the Dead festival honors the spirits of those who have passed away. On this day, Mexicans decorate the graves of their loved ones with "bread for the dead," a symbolic gesture to their well-being in the afterlife.

FEASTS AND FIESTAS

E ver since baskets of tamales circulated at Aztec banquets, Mexican food has meant life, happiness, and celebration. The Mexican people find much cause for rejoicing. Mexico observes 15 national holidays and countless local festivals and fiestas. No family milestone--whether a christening, graduation, planting, wedding, First Communion, birthday, saint's day, or funeral--passes without a party and feasting. In addition, any workday that falls between two holidays, becomes a *puente*, a day of rest.

The word "fiesta" comes from the Latin *festa*, meaning joyous. A fiesta provides a break from everyday life and an occasion to honor family, friends, church, or country. Just as native Mexican cuisine blended with influences of other cultures, fiestas may reflect the coming together of ancient ritual, Spanish culture, and Christian religion. A solemn occasion may be marked by a colorful explosion of merriment—music, dancing, costumes. Always, good food abounds.

Roman Catholicism remains the predominant Mexican faith. Every city, town, and village holds a fiesta to honor its patron saint's day and give thanks for protection and blessings. Traditionally, a prosperous local businessman or farmer sponsors the fiesta. Supplying the meat or other food represents a privilege and

42

a way to thank God for good fortune. Festivities take place in the neighborhood plaza, the heart of the community. Businesses close for anywhere from one day to a week while festivities are underway. Celebrations may involve masks, costumes, pageants, bullfights, a pilgrimage, a special religious service, games, horsemanship, fireworks, singing, dancing, or giant puppets. Food vendors set up booths nearby.

A unique Mexican holiday blending ancient ritual with religious elements is the Day of the Dead, *El Día de los Muertos*. Despite its grim-sounding name, this happy holiday actually embraces life by honoring ancestors. The festival lasts three days, October 31 through November 2, the same days as All Hallows Eve, All Saints Day, and All Souls Day.

Long ago, the Aztecs believed success in life required showing proper respect for the dead. To help souls journey to Mictlán, their land of the dead, they built shrines on which they placed images of the departed and offerings of fruit and flowers. Today, during the Day of the Dead, Mexicans heap gifts to

Sugar skulls and other candy are used to decorate altars for the Day of the Dead festival, which is observed during the fall.

Mexican cuisine is often colorful, due to the combinations of ripe vegetables, meat, and tortillas that are part of almost every meal.

deceased loved ones on homemade altars. They await the return of their ancestors' souls to earth for one day. Skulls, crossbones, and skeletons, symbols of life in ancient Mexico, appear as figures, costumes, masks, and candy.

Day of the Dead celebrations vary through different regions of Mexico. In some villages, families build altars for their offerings—*ofrendas*—in their homes. Local church bells ring to summon returning souls, and fireworks explode to welcome them. In other places, Mexican families travel to graveyards on October 31 and stay through the entire holiday. There, they build altars and stack them with religious statues, poems, candles, and gifts of favorite foods and objects their loved one enjoyed in life. Bright bundles of flowers—yellow marigolds the Aztecs called *zempoalxóchitl*, known in Mexico as the flower of the dead; bright red *terciopelo*, or cockscomb; and baby's breath—also top these altars. Food offerings frequently include tamales, molé, fruit, hot chocolate, and a special holiday bread, *pan de muertos*.

"Bread for the dead" is one variety of Mexico's hundreds of *pan dulces* (sweet breads). Bakeries prepare it especially for the holiday. Round loaves are

Red beans, sold here from a sack in a market stall, round out a healthy Mexican meal. They can be eaten with rice, or included in the filling for tortillas.

coated with licorice-flavored sugary syrup and decorated with crossbones. Some families order one loaf baked for each deceased relative. Sometimes homemade papier-mâché faces are tucked into the loaves.

Another Day of the Dead specialty, *calaveras,* are molded sugar figures decorated with colored icing. Children write their names on sugar skulls and place them on the altars. Artists in Toluca, Mexico, begin working as early as May each year to create skull-, animal-, flower-, or coffin-shaped sugar figures. Through a process called *alfeñique,* they shape a mixture of sugar, egg whites, and food coloring in clay molds. Once the figures dry and harden, they are painted with icing.

On November 1, after a light breakfast, families tend gravesites. They may share their evening meal of tamales and molé with departed loved ones by placing portions on the altars. Throughout that night they hold candlelight vigils, praying and burning incense, while awaiting the returning souls. Food vendors set up stalls nearby. The spirits of the dead are believed to return and join the festivities on November 2. The celebration peaks with picnics, bands, balloons, songs, games, and fireworks.

As important as the Day of the Dead is to Mexican culture, Christmas is Mexico's most important holiday. The traditional Mexican Christmas celebration begins with Las Posadas on December 16 and lasts through the Epiphany on January 6. On December 16, Mexican families display elaborate nativity sets. Figures collected over many years may represent a tiny village with details like tiny cactus plants. The nativity may even include a figurine depicting a woman kneeling at a

According to custom, *buñuelos* purchased at sidewalk stands in Oaxaca are served in pottery dishes. Once the pancakes are eaten, the dishes are smashed.

45

metate making tortillas. According to tradition, the baby Jesus figure is not placed in the manger until December 24.

December 16 also begins the first of nine symbolic processions combining religion and fun. These are called *Posadas* (meaning "refuges" or "shelters"). Local processions portray Mary and Joseph's journey from Nazareth to Bethlehem. Along the way, the participants sing hymns and knock on doors. At each stop, they are turned away until they reach their true destination. Here, a party is planned. Along with holiday foods, tamales, **buñuelos**, hot chocolate, and cakes, there may be fireworks. Blindfolded children swing sticks to break open a piñata. The decorated papier-mâché piñatas are filled with small sweets, cookies, peanuts, and fruit.

In Mexico, as most places, Christmas means making favorite dishes from old family recipes. Festive foods vary between regions and individual families. Entire families may pitch in to fry batches of buñuelos. These Christmas treats are

Bacalao is a popular dish made with cod, a type of fish that can be caught along the coast of Mexico.

(Right) An agave plant thrives in the desert of Baja California Sur. Sap from the leaves of the agave can be distilled to make tequila, a popular alcoholic drink.

(Bottom) Workers cut agave plants at the La Rojena tequila distillery in Jalisco. The distillery opened in 1812, making it the oldest active distillery in Latin America. The La Rojena facility is owned by the Jose Cuervo corporation.

Tamales are served at most Mexican festivals and fiestas.

48

sometimes exchanged as gifts.

Christmas Eve and Christmas Day mean a quiet celebration at home. Families share a Christmas Eve dinner, attend midnight mass, and exchange presents. The American customs of decorating a tree, exchanging gifts on Christmas, and roasting a turkey have only recently become popular. While wild turkey is native to Mexico, holiday turkey has usually been served as molé poblano.

Other traditional Christmas dishes include *bacalao*, an extravagant European creation of dried cod soaked, reconstituted, and baked with oil and spices in a slow oven; *revoltijo*, dried shrimp patties and vegetables cooked in molé; and *pierna*, leg of pork. Flavored with sugar, cinnamon, or mint and fruits such as oranges, strawberries, and lime, *Ponche de Navidad* (Christmas punch) is served warm or over ice. The colorful Christmas Eve salad, *Ensalada de Noche Buena*, contains beets, *jícama*, oranges, and peanuts. While many Mexican dishes are garnished with vegetables, this ranks as probably the only authentic Mexican salad. Americans invented taco salad.

The custom of serving tamales at all Mexican celebrations dates back perhaps as far as A.D. 750. Making tamales requires so much time and work, they are usually prepared at home only for special celebrations. Families or neighbors line up to cook in assembly-line fashion. Normally, a mixture of corn dough, broth, chili sauce, and chopped meat or beans is wrapped in cornhusks, which are folded and steamed. Tamales differ according to tastes and regions. They may be wrapped in banana leaves instead of cornhusks or flavored with molé. Fillings might be made from beef, pork, shrimp, fish, pumpkin, pineapple, or even wild cherries. Sweet tamales with raisins, candied fruit, cinnamon, or pecans are preferred in some regions, especially at Christmastime. Some tamales contain no filling.

Since ancient times, the beverages *pulque* or *atole* were always served with tamales. Now considered old-fashioned, that custom has been abandoned for modern drinks such as soda or coffee.

The Christmas holidays end on January 6. Figurines of baby Jesus are hidden in the *Rosca de los Reyes* (Bread of the Kings) a ring-shaped sweet bread. Whoever finds the doll must host a party with dancing and molé on February 2, *Día de Candelaria*.

TEXT-DEPENDENT QUESTIONS

When is the Day of the Dead celebrated?

What are some of the foods often served during the Christmas season in Mexico?

RESEARCH PROJECT

The Quinceañera, or 15th birthday celebration for young women, is observed by Mexican families, as well as others of Hispanic descent in the United States and Latin America. Using the Internet, find out how the Quinceañera is celebrated in Mexico. What are some foods that are commonly enjoyed at this fiesta?

 WORDS TO UNDERSTAND

entrepreneur—a businessperson who launches new enterprises.

flan—a custard baked with a caramel glaze.

5

In Mexico, most families eat a large meal in the early afternoon and four smaller meals at different times during the day.

FIVE MEALS A DAY
AND BETWEEN-MEAL WHIMS

A Mexican saying, *"se me antojó,"* describes a sudden, fanciful craving for a snack. The best known of all Mexican foods, *antojitos* are literally "little whims." Usually antojitos mean corn-based items, the tacos, chalupas, and enchiladas so familiar to Americans. In Mexico, these treats are sold by vendors or in small restaurants called *taquerías*.

Mexican food vendors set up stalls wherever a crowd will gather. Pushcarts become part of every festival or fiesta. Vendors may do business near the entrance of a public building or outside the church on a feast day. Back in colonial times, resourceful women supported their families by cooking enchiladas or quesadillas over a charcoal brazier on a street corner and selling them to passersby. In modern times, street-corner cooks continue to do business.

 If you carve a pumpkin next Halloween, save the seeds to try this snack. Wash the seeds well, then spread them in one layer on a cookie sheet. Roast them in the oven at 375°F (191°C) for 20 to 30 minutes to dry. Dot them with butter or margarine and return them to the oven for 5 to 10 minutes, stirring frequently until toasted. Sprinkle with salt. Cool and eat. Store leftovers in a sealed jar.

Flan is a popular dish in Mexico. As a dessert, it is often served with fresh fruit like oranges and blackberries.

Buying food from stalls first became popular during the Spanish colonial period. Ordinary Mexicans loved tamales and other traditional foods, but the upper classes scorned traditional food as the preference of commoners. They hired French or Chinese cooks and ate European dishes. For them, eating tamales was acceptable only in secret, at home alone.

During the 1800s, families invented special country picnics as an excuse to eat tamales. Clever **entrepreneurs** also decided travel provided a good excuse to indulge in favorite foods. They sold tamales from roadside stands and later in railroad stations. Parties where only tamales and hot chocolate or coffee were served were known as *tamaladas*.

Antojitos can also be served as appetizers before *la comida*, the day's main meal. Some antojitos are less familiar to Americans than tacos or tamales, or they vary from our Americanized

 Through geographic regions of Mexico, food varies according to available local products and cultural influences. Until 1910, most Americans knew only the dishes prepared close to home. When they traveled to fight in the Mexican Revolution, they were exposed to new foods they had never tried before.

A vendor prepares quesadillas at a food stand in the Merced Market in Mexico City.

versions. A true Mexican taco is seldom crunchy and consists of meat, cheese, potatoes, or other food wrapped in a soft corn or flour tortilla. Americans eat enchiladas as a main course, but in Mexico, they are considered snacks. A Mexican quesadilla is a tortilla filled with cheese, mushrooms, pork, or squash blossoms, then grilled. Tostadas resemble those we know, fried corn tortillas topped with beans, lettuce, and other garnishes. Other antojitos strike Americans as less familiar: *sopes,* small corn cakes filled with bean paste, and *molotes*, fried corn pancakes stuffed with cheese and chilies.

In addition to antojitos, sidewalk vendors sell many other treats: *tortas*, popular Mexican sandwiches; peanuts coated with chile; acorns; cucumber chunks; hot roasted chestnuts; roasted yams; roasted ears of corn with mayonnaise, cheese, and powdered chile, or lime juice and powdered chile; beans; soda, **flan**, or rice pudding. They also sell fruit ices made of mangoes, coconut, or peaches mixed with sugar, packed in ice, and spun into slush. Hot or cold pumpkinseeds, shelled or unshelled, fried, toasted or salted, also rank among the favorites.

Traditionally, Mexicans eat five daily meals: a large one at midday and four light meals or snacks. Dinner, *la comida*, constitutes the day's important meal, traditionally enjoyed at home with family. The five standard courses begin with soup, followed by a "dry soup" (rice or macaroni), then meat or fish with vegetables and tortillas, beans, and finally a dessert of pudding or fruit, and coffee. In changing times, the bean course is frequently skipped.

A woman sells homemade tacos from a market stall in a Mexican plaza. Deep-fried "hard-shell" tacos are rarely eaten in Mexico; the soft tortilla has traditionally been used to prepare tacos.

Today's busy schedules, especially in large cities, no longer allow the luxury of a *siesta* or nap after dinner. Once, most individuals rested at home through the hottest part of the day and returned to work around 7:00 in the evening. Mealtimes have shifted to meet the demands of modern life.

Days once began with an early light breakfast of rolls and hot chocolate or coffee and fruit, followed by a more substantial brunch of eggs or meat. Today breakfast in Mexico might entail coffee, eggs, and corn flakes. Light fare in late afternoon, similar to what the English eat at teatime, curbs appetites between lunch and dinner. *Cena* or supper comes late by our standards, at 9 or 10 o'clock at night.

Just as food varies between regions of the United States—lobster rolls in New England to grits in the South—local products and cultural influences differ throughout Mexico. Rustic flavors are a trademark of Northern Mexico. Flour tortillas are more common in central Mexico. Cooking in the West Central is the least traditional, reflecting heavy outside influences. In southern Mexico and the Yucatán peninsula, tropical fruits, vegetables, and seafood are popular. Oaxaca retains much of its Amerindian heritage when it comes to food.

Mexican shoppers today appreciate the convenience of purchasing frozen and ready-made foods in supermarkets. Modern chain stores offer international foods—sushi, pizza, and French bread. Most fresh foods—tortillas, meat, and produce—are purchased from food stalls, handcarts, or at outdoor markets. Market vendors sell meat, cheese, fruit, vegetables and ready-to-eat tamales, atole, tacos, sandwiches, fruit drinks, enchiladas, and soup.

 Before stores existed in Mexico, open-air markets provided a place to trade or sell goods. Today Mexican markets open once a week in rural villages and daily in cities. Vendors offer fresh food and colorful handicrafts.

People sit outside a McDonald's restaurant in downtown Mexico City. Fast food has become very popular in Mexico because of its low cost and quick service. Unfortunately, this has contributed to the rising rate of obesity in the country. By 2014, Mexico had surpassed the United States as the world's "fattest" nation, with an adult obesity rate of 32.8 percent, according to a report by the United Nations Food and Agricultural Organization.

A variety of restaurants and cafeterias operate in Mexico, and family celebrations today are sometimes held in restaurants. Mexico City offers international dining—German, Japanese, Italian, French, Chinese. Fast food has also arrived in the land of the Aztecs: the first McDonald's restaurant opened in

October 1985. Now the chain has more than 500 restaurants throughout the country. Since the government eased restrictions on foreign restaurant companies, many other chains have expanded into the country, including American companies like Denny's, Burger King, and Subway are also located in Mexico City.

Mexican outdoor markets are called *tianguis*, named for the canvas or plastic tarps spread on the ground and overhead.

57

Mexican cuisine has come a long way since the Aztecs, but their techniques for making tortillas and tamales have endured through the centuries. Despite the creation of new dishes through the influence of many cultures, one aspect remains the same. Today, as in ancient times, the food of Mexico represents a glorious celebration of life.

TEXT-DEPENDENT QUESTIONS

What food and drink is served at a *tamalada* party?

What is the main meal of the day called in Mexico?

RESEARCH PROJECT

Many public health experts are concerned about the rising rate of obesity in Mexico, which they believe is linked to another issue facing the country—the high rate of poverty and the growing disparity between the wealthy and poor citizens. Do some research on this issue, and write an essay either supporting or rejecting the link between these issues. Cite data and statistics to back up your conclusion.

SERIES GLOSSARY

adobe—a building material made of mud and straw.

Amerindian—a term for the indigenous peoples of North and South America before the arrival of Europeans in the late 15th century.

conquistador—any one of the Spanish leaders of the conquest of the Americas in the 1500s.

criollo—a resident of New Spain who was born in North America to parents of Spanish ancestry. In the social order of New Spain, criollos ranked above mestizos.

fiesta—a Mexican party or celebration.

haciendas—large Mexican ranches.

maquiladoras—factories created to attract foreign business to Mexico by allowing them to do business cheaply.

mariachi—a Mexican street band that performs a distinctive type of music utilizing guitars, violins, and trumpets.

Mesoamerica—the region of southern North America that was inhabited before the arrival of the Spaniards.

mestizo—a person of mixed Amerindian and European (typically Spanish) descent.

Nahuatl—the ancient language spoken by the Aztecs; still spoken by many modern Mexicans.

New Spain—name for the Spanish colony that included modern-day Mexico. This vast area of North America was conquered by Spain in the 1500s and ruled by the Spanish until 1821.

plaza—the central open square at the center of Spanish cities in Mexico.

pre-Columbian—referring to a time before the 1490s, when Christopher Columbus landed in the Americas.

FURTHER READING

Gritzner, Charles F. *Mexico*. New York: Chelsea House, 2012.

Kent, Deborah. *Mexico*. New York: Children's Press, 2012.

Kennedy, Diana. *The Essential Cuisines of Mexico*. New York: Clarkston Potter, 2000.

Long-Solis, Janet, and Luis Alberto Vargas. *Food Culture in Mexico*. Westport, Conn.: Greenwood Press, 2005.

Mayor, Guy. *Mexico: A Quick Guide to Customs and Etiquette*. New York: Kuperard, 2006.

Peterson, Joan. *Eat Smart in Mexico*. Corte Madera: Ginko Press, 2008.

Sterling, David. *Yucatán: Recipes from a Culinary Expedition*. Austin: University of Texas Press, 2014.

Santibanez, Roberto, with J.J. Goode. *Tacos, Tortas, and Tamales: Flavors from the Griddles, Pots, and Streetside Kitchens of Mexico*. New York: Houghton Mifflin, 2014.

INTERNET RESOURCES

Mexican recipies
http://mexican.food.com

Cookbook author Jim Peyton discusses Mexican food and cooking.
www.lomexicano.com

Mexican Cuisine, from the University of Guadalajara
www.mexico.udg.mx/cocina/ingles/ingles.html

Mesoweb
http://www.mesoweb.com/welcome.html#externalresources

National Geographic
http://kids.nationalgeographic.com/kids/places/find/mexico

CIA World Factbook, facts about Mexico
https://www.cia.gov/library/publications/the-world-factbook/geos/mx.html

INDEX

Aztecs, 11, 12–21, 23, 24, 32, 41, 42, 45, 57

Centéotl (god of the harvest), 15, 16
Chicomecóatl (goddess of sustenance), 16
Christianity, 20, 31, 41
Christmas, 31, 39, 40, 45, 46, 48, 49
Communion, 37, 41
Convent of San Francisco, 31
Cortés, Hernán, 15, 19, 20

Day of the Dead, 42–45

Easter, 31
Epiphany, 45

Frito-Lay, 23

genetically modified (GMO) corn, 29
Greenpeace, 29

Jalisco, 47

La Malinche (Doña Marina), 19
La Rojena tequila distillery, 47
Lake Texcoco, 18
Las Posadas, 46

Maya, 16, 23
McDonald's, 56–57
Mexican food
    antojitos, 12, 51–54
    bacalao, 46
    bread for the dead, 41, 43–44
    buñuelos, 45, 46–47
    calaveras, 45
    camote, 31, 39
    chilies, 11, 15, 20, 35, 36, 37
    enchilada, 12, 51, 53, 55
    huevos rancheros, 9

marzipan, 31, 39
molé poblano, 32, 35–36, 48
pulque, 15, 49
quesadilla, 12, 51, 53
taco, 11, 12, 23, 48, 51, 52, 53, 54, 55
tamale, 11, 12, 16, 20, 21, 24, 37, 41, 45,
    46, 49, 52, 53, 57
tortilla, 11, 12, 15, 16, 19, 21, 23–29, 36,
    46, 54, 55, 57
tostada, 23, 53
white pozole (pozole blanco), 38
and rising obesity rate in Mexico, 56

Mictlán, 42
Monterrey, 37
Montezuma II, 18, 19, 20, 21
Morales, Francisco "Frank," 11

Nahuatl, 19
NASA, 24

Oaxaca, 39, 45, 55

Puebla, 31, 35, 39

Quetzalcoatl, 18

Santa Rosa convent, 31, 35
Sor Andrea de la Asuncíon, 35
Spanish explorers, 12, 18–19, 37, 52

Tenochtitlán (Mexico City), 15, 18, 19, 32, 57
Tlascalan, 19
Toluca, 45

Xilonen
    See Chicomecóatl

Yucatán Peninsula, 15, 55

PICTURE CREDITS

ABOUT THE AUTHOR

Jan McDaniel is a former newspaper reporter and the author of more than 20 novels. She and her husband live in Chattanooga, Tennessee.